STRONGER, BETTER, WISER

WALK INTO THE NEW YOU

Simone Williams-Young
Reuben L. Young Sr.
Dr. Angela Roberson
Brenda J. Williams
Temika McCann
James Hewitt

Young at Heart Publishing LLC.

Copyright © 2023 All Authors

All rights reserved.

No portion of this book may be reproduced in any form without written permission from the publisher or author, except as permitted by U.S. copyright law.

To request permission contact

ISBN: 979-8-9898143-0-5

ISBN: 979-8-9898143-1-2

Printed in United States of America

Published by: Young at Heart Publishing LLC.

Publisher's Foreword

Thank you for choosing to read this book from Young at Heart Publishing LLC. This is a special project for us, as it is the first book we have published and the first collaboration we have facilitated. We are proud of the result and hope you will enjoy it as much as we did. This is just the beginning of our journey, and we look forward to bringing you more quality books in the future.

This collaboration, "Stronger, Better, Wiser: Walk Into the New You," is a collection of inspiring stories that I was guided to compile. God revealed to me that many people are trapped in the past, and God has greater plans for His people, but He requires us to leave behind the old so that He can grant us the "New."

I am so proud of the co-authors who stepped up to the plate, rolled up their sleeves, and allowed the Holy Spirit to impart in them a word for the people. This is a collaboration that encourages with biblical principles to apply for your daily use. These are testimonial stories that you can identify and know that you are not alone.

At Young at Heart Publishing LLC, we believe in the power of books to inspire and empower people. We are committed to helping aspiring authors share their stories and insights with the world. Whether you have a personal journey, professional expertise, or a creative vision, we are here to support you and make your dream come true.

Stronger, Better, Wiser: Walk into the New You, is a book that offers practical and spiritual guidance for transforming your life. We hope that you will find this book helpful and uplifting and that it will motivate you to pursue your goals and passions.

Thank you for choosing Young at Heart Publishing LLC. We wish you all the best.

Simone Williams-Young
CEO and Founder Young at Heart Publishing LLC
www.Yahpublish.com

Table of Contents

New Covenant 1

No time for the past! 9
    Time is of the essence! 13
    Rule your emotions! 15
    Do not turn to salt! 18
    Do not bring the Old to the New! 21
    Fight! Your life depends on it! 24
    Simone Williams-Young 29

Stronger Together 32
    Two people are better than one! 33
    The Esther Anointing 36
    Dr. Angela Roberson 42

Executing Wisdom Destroys the Foolishness in Life 46
    Brenda J. Williams 61

The Power of Your Inner Strength 63
    Self-Reflection, Isolation, and Re-focus 66
    Self-Denial, Self-Destruction, & Distraction 70
    Reuben L. Young Sr. 77

Be Authentic 79
    Let's Break This Thing Down 80

Be Yourself.. 86

Always Be True.. 87

Temika McCann... 91

Better Because of It 93

James Hewitt... 110

Senior Pastor

Chief Apostle Michael L. Rowles

Wrecking Crew for Christ Holiness Church

11250 S. Avalon Boulevard

Los Angeles, CA 90061

This chapter is a transcribed message from Sunday Morning Service, January 7, 2024, used with permission from Chief Apostle Michael L Rowles.

A special thank you to my Chief Apostle for allowing me to include the message God gave him to release to the people in this book. I felt it would bless many because the message was right in line with what had already been written. This is a prophetic message and if applied it will add great change to your life. I pray that this message encourages you helps strengthen your faith in God and pushes you to walk in the NEW.

NEW COVENANT

(Walking In Your New)

Isaiah 42:6 NIV reads:

"I, the Lord, have called you in righteousness; I will take hold of your hand. I will keep you and will make you to be a covenant for the people and a light for the Gentiles.

God told me to tell you this year he has made a New covenant with the people.

Isaiah 42:8 KJV reads:

"I am the LORD: that is my name: and my glory will I not give to another, neither my praise to graven images"

He will not give us the glory, but we can wear his glory, I can see the glory on the people of God, but it is covering the people.

Isaiah 42:9 KJV reads:

"Behold, the former things are come to pass, and new things do I declare before they spring forth, I tell you of them."

We are a lively stone; this is where God wants you to come alive. This is where you get rid of the dead weight and come alive. The individual may not understand your shout or the praise, it is because of the confidence and the trust you have in your God.

Behold the former things are come to pass. Everything God has promised you in 2024 has come to pass, and new things do I declare. New things are going to happen to you. That is why the enemy knows that God has spoken and when God speaks something, it will not return void. When God speaks something, you must Believe God. You must allow yourself to think new things and what God is about to do. Behold the former things are come to pass but new things I do declare before thee, and they should spring forth and I will tell you about them. I stopped by to tell you of the things that are about to happen. Things God is about to work that miracle that you have been praying. For God delights in his elect. When you trust the God that you serve and believe in God's Word, it is time to speak new things and start speaking those things and making those things come to pass. The Bible says in KJV Romans 4:17-19 reads:

[17] As it is written, I have made thee a father of many nations, before him whom he believed, even God, who quickened the dead, and calleth those things which be not as though they were.

¹⁸ Who against hope believed in hope, that he might become the father of many nations, according to that which was spoken, so shall thy seed be.

¹⁹ And being not weak in faith, he considered not his own body now dead, when he was about a hundred years old, neither yet the deadness of Sarah's womb:

To call them to pass you must walk in the path of righteousness and believe God at his Word. You must decree things in your life, you must not allow the mind to play games with you. That is why the bible says in Philippians Chapter 2:5. "**Let this mind be in you, which was also in Christ Jesus**. It is time to regulate your mind because your mind setting determines your blessing." You must not allow the enemy to keep taking you down memory lane. **Isaiah 43:18** KJV says, "Remember ye, not the former things, neither consider the things of old." Tell yourself I have a new mind and a new way of thinking. I refuse to think like I used to think because all it has done is set me back and put me in a place of stagnation. It is time for you to declare the blessings of God. The word of God says to call those things which be not as though they are. You have to start speaking stuff in existence. The Bible says so as a man thinketh so is he. It is time to start speaking positively because negative will throw you off. That is why the Bible says in James 1:8 "A **double-minded man**, is unstable in all his ways." It is time for you to start speaking positively in your life. God says stop telling yourself I am sick instead, tell yourself I am well. Start telling yourself, "I can do all things through Christ that strengthens me." You must understand your mind must develop in the conscious of God and you must believe God gave us the power to decree and declare these things in your life. You must speak to yourself and tell yourself I am not the same person; I am not like I used to be, do not act like that anymore. Get in charge of your life, stop letting the devil play with your mind. He will not overtake you when you speak positive things against him. You must understand that this is the year God set aside just for you and you must believe it, for the bible says. **Isaiah 43:1** NKJV But now, thus says the LORD, who created you, O Jacob, And He who formed you, O Israel: "Fear not, for I have redeemed you; I have called you by your name; You are Mine." You must let the devil know that I am God's Child, and you are a lie from the pits of hell. You will not make me, lead me, deceive me, or overtake me. That is why he said to cast down every imagination. You must cast them down. It is time to take authority over that thought and put that thought in its right place and not allow it to overtake your thoughts. Because a good man thinks good, and an evil man speaks evil. When you are thinking that God has given me the power you must also tell yourself the bible says new things that I declare. I declare new things over your life, I declare a new mind setting, I declare a new residence, I declare a new mind, I declare a new relationship, I declare new joy, I declare new vision, I declare release, I declare new health. When a king declares and decrees something It must happen, it must come to pass when you decree it. That is why he says I declare before thee, for I should tell you of things of them. I stopped by to tell you, that you will be fortunate, you will succeed, you will prosper in the things of God; You will make it in your life, and you will live and not die. For God delights in His elect who

God has chosen to open the blind eyes of them in prison, for God came to set the captives free. One thing about God, when you decree it and declare it the word of God works. KJV John 1:1 reads, In the beginning was the word and the word was with God, and the word was God. KJV John 1:14 reads, and the word was made flesh, and dwelt among us (and we beheld His glory, the glory as of the only begotten of the Father,) full of grace and truth. KJV John 15:7 reads: If ye abide in me, and my words abide in you, ye shall ask what ye will, and it shall be done unto you. When you stand on His Word, He will give you what your heart desires. You must start speaking new and get away from the old songs. You must stop allowing yourself to say I am nobody; No, say I am somebody, I decree and declare it. You must say, I will make it, my children will make it, my family will make it, my neighborhood will make it, I receive my benefits.

KJV 43:1 says, but now, thus saith the Lord that created thee, O Jacob, and he who formed thee. Oh Israel: "Fear Not, for I have redeemed thee; I have called thee by thy name, thou are mine." God has called you out of that condition and the enemy wants to manipulate you. The Word of God says, "Fear thou not for I am with thee; be not dismayed neither be afraid for I am thy God; I will help thee; yea I will uphold thee with thy right hand." Someone needs to know this is a coming out year for you. This is a year of new covenant, new connections, new places, new property, and new mindsets. You must say to yourself, I will walk in righteousness and my newness when hen the enemy has tried to get me to sing a sad song but sing unto the lord a new song and His praises from the end of the earth ye that go down to the sea, and all that is therein the isles, and the inhabitants thereof. I will do newness, I speak it; I walk it. I do not see an old house; I see a new house. I don't see an old car I see a new car; I don't see old friends, I see new friends; I don't see an old church, I see a new church; I don't see an old phase I see a new phase, I don't see an old shout I see a new shout; I don't see old ways I see new ways. Say New! It's imperative that you begin a new relationship with yourself, a new journey; because now it is time to see the new things that I declare that things are getting ready to happen in your favor. The old business is not going to be able to succeed in your new business, my new book and my new chapter are my best chapter because my old chapter has been closed to start my new book. Somebody is not going to like the new you and that's their prerogative if they don't like who you are about to become because I'm about to become everything God wants me to be. Because you are just starting brand new, that's why you cannot afford to let anyone come to you with old stuff. Tell them old things have passed away and behold all things become new. Whenever you start your new journey old people will start to pop up because it is only to try and throw you off because of what is about to happen. I release to you to recognize it in the name of Jesus because of what God is about to do. You cannot be entangled in that old stuff that had you bound; had you down; had you upset, but now I'm about to see brand new things. God wants you to have that new mindset because you won't be able to succeed. **Matthew 9:17** talks about how you cannot put old wines into new wineskins, and you cannot put new wines into old wineskin. You have to quit trying to make old stuff work when God is trying to do a new thing.

You have to let it go because you are worth more than that. God is about to complete His investments this year in this season. This is the 7th day of completion of walking in your new season. You have to leave all the weight and all the pain. You cannot even carry some folk this year, you have to let them go. You have to shake them off and say I am sorry; I am tired of that old song; you do not want to move forward. You want to continue to tell me everything that is happening that is going to keep still happening. You are going to still do the same thing if you don't make changes. It's time to do something different in your life. You cannot keep complaining about why this is not happening, and why is God not coming through because if you keep doing the same thing you going to get the same results. You do the same thing then blame God. No! This year you need to make some changes. This year! Say this year I'm making some changes. Some people are going to be mad because you're going to have to shift them. All you do is bring me all this pain, and I refuse to contaminate my spirit and hold all this stuff and you do not want to do anything about it. I can understand people who want to change conversation but all you want to do is harvest on everything that is happening that you are not trying to change. You will continue to stay stuck doing the same thing when God says I declare I will do a new thing, but God is not a forceful God, He gives you your own choices and decisions. If you like it, I love it! It is time for you to make conscious decisions this year. Now is not the time to play the blame game. God will bless you even in your shame. But it is time to stop playing the blame game and try to blame somebody for something you will not do. Because you are in the same predicament and situation because you want to continue to live the same life, and want to do the same thing, by now you would think if nothing happened then, then nothing is going to happen now. I'm going to shift this; I am going to make a conscious decision starting today on what I need to do with my life. I refuse to be broke, I refuse to be hungry, I refuse to be homeless, I refuse to hang with people who talk about me. The theme is the "clean-up" man. I come to clean up and tell the devil enough is enough. I refuse to sit here and not do something with my life. Say, "I am somebody, I know who I am, and if you do not think so, I do not have to be validated by anyone and I will regulate my life." It is time to do something new. God said because some of us started on the wrong foot this year he said today to get on the good foot! It is time to see things from a different perspective in the things of God.

No time for the past!

Simone Williams-Young

New day, new time, new year, new grace, new mercies, new life, new love, fresh anointing, new vision be unto you in Jesus' name.

Lamentations 3:22-23

²²"Through the Lord's mercies we are not consumed, Because His compassions fail not." ²³They are new every morning; Great is Your faithfulness."

No more stagnation, self-doubt, self-sabotage, low self-esteem, indecisiveness, procrastination, self-worthlessness, and any of those things that keep us from moving into our "New." God said that we were made for His glory. These negative things we allow to keep us from moving forward are not bringing Him glory; they are doing the contrary.

Time is valuable; once it has gone, you cannot get it back. In our new season, we are going to leave behind all things that are holding us back. **WE DO NOT HAVE TIME FOR THAT!** "What do you mean by 'In your New'?" Well, I am glad you asked! When God allows you to wake up in the morning, this is a new day.

A new chance to change, repent, make amends with loved ones, and create a new action plan to get back on track with God in your personal life and with yourself. Even if you were not doing your best at your work, a new day allows you to do better to reach a new goal, a new day to challenge yourself, a new day to do something you have never done before. Every time you wake up to take another breath, it is a new day to reinvent yourself. Yesterday was the old me; today is the new me because I have a much better perspective on my goals and what I want to achieve. Your past does not define your future, but it can be used to make you stronger, better, and wiser. That is where you take all of your experience—the good, the bad, and the ugly—and use it to work for you.

Do you know that sometimes you can turn your pain, passions, and life lessons into a business, a book, or a movie, or simply use them to help someone else pull through a situation like yours? Even though some situations may be unpleasant, uncomfortable, or simply painful, God knows how to use everything and turn it around for our good. For example, my son was killed on August 1, 2020. It was devastating and very painful during that time. It also showed me how much stronger I was through God's help. I was able to turn that experience and put it into a book called *"I Choose to Live: Pushing Through the Grieving Process."* Many people have come back and said how they enjoyed the book and how it has helped them with their grieving or reached out to me for advice through their grieving process. Never would I have imagined that I would become an author and now write this, my second book in this collaboration. All I have to say is God is amazing and He will lead you in the right direction.

Romans 8:28:

"And we know that in all things God works for the good of those who love him, who have been called according to His purpose."

Time is of the essence!

What is time? Definition:
*The indefinite continued progress of existence and events
in the past, present, and future regarded as a whole*

Every moment and every second seems to be moving faster and faster. If we do not learn to take control over our emotions, thoughts, and habits, soon we will look up and wonder where the time went and why we are still stuck in the same place and not further advancing.

In Ecclesiastes 3:1,
*the Word of God says, "To everything there is a season,
a time for every purpose under heaven:"*

In this verse, if you read the entire chapter, it lets us know that there is a time and a season for everything we do. Each season has a beginning and an end. We cannot stay in that season forever; there will never be any progression. We know we are born and live only so long on the earth. You can plant a seed, and it will grow. There will also be an end date for that seed that was planted. What we do with the time from the beginning to the end is crucial on this earth. It is what I like to call the in-between time. No one knows when the day of expiration of anything will come. The important thing is what we do with the time that we are given to nurture the gifts that God has given us. We must value the ideas He has placed in us or even nurture and value the people He has placed in our lives. God may only give us grace for something for a period of time. If we squander or misuse that time and the expiration date of a thing comes up, then here we go, begging for more time because we just noticed or realized the value of it. Then it is no one's fault but our own!

Rule your emotions!

So many of us have heard the cliche saying, "Let the past be the past," but it is necessary in the journey of new beginnings. The past is part of our history, and there is nothing that we could ever do to change it, but we should press towards the things ahead of us and not what is behind us.

Philippians 3:13 says,

"Brethren, I count not myself to have apprehended: but this one thing I do, forgetting those things which are behind, and reaching forth unto those things which are before, ¹⁴ I press toward the mark for the prize of the high calling of God in Christ Jesus."

When we keep reaching into our past, chances are we will pull out something we do not need. Reaching into our past is like putting our hands in a grab bag, not knowing what the surprise is going to be. Often, things people do or say can be a trigger to an emotion from the past. I will never forget that my husband made a harmless comment that was meant to be funny, but instead, for a moment, it brought back a feeling or an emotion from my past, even a memory. He even noticed that I got quiet and withdrawn for a moment. It reminded me of how, at times, men treated me in the past and what they would say to me. That statement would make me feel low and worthless. I felt it implied that men would not do something for me without them wanting something in return. At that moment, I had a choice to continue to withdraw and go down memory lane or to remember it was my husband with whom I was speaking, the man that I know means me no harm or evil. He is the person who has always encouraged me and brought me out of my shell of the broken place that I used to be in.

If I had let that emotion from the past fester and grow, that could have placed a wedge between us. I did not keep my feelings to myself and made sure that I communicated with my husband. My husband was able to bring me out of that mental space and help replace that feeling with love, compassion, and understanding. I also began to pray and cast those emotions down because I refused to keep going down memory lane. I know who I am now, and I will not let the past dictate how my future or relationship with my husband will be. 2 Corinthians 10:5 says to "Cast down imaginations, and every high thing that exalted itself against the knowledge of God and bringing into captivity every thought to the obedience of Christ."

People of God, we need to walk in the "New." More than ever before, we need to stop letting our past dictate our future. God wishes for us to prosper and be in good health. When we continue to focus and stay fixated on the past, it can take a toll on our physical and mental health. If our minds are so weighed down with the emotions that focusing on the path brings, we will not truly be able to focus on the greatness in us. The Bible says, "Greater is He who lives in us than He that is in the world" (1 John 4:4). We will not recognize that we are great because we will not be able to truly focus on Him.

DO NOT TURN TO SALT!

When I look at Lot and his wife in Genesis Chapter 19, it begins to tell a story of how they lived in Sodom and Gomorrah. This city was filled with all sorts of wickedness and immorality that was not pleasing to God.

Because of the people's wickedness, God decided to destroy this city and everyone in it but decided to spare Lot and his family.

Genesis 19: 12-13

12 "The two men said to Lot, Do you have anyone else here—sons- in-law, sons or daughters, or anyone else in the city who belongs to you?

Get them out of here,

13 because we are going to destroy this place. The outcry to the Lord against its people is so great that he has sent us to destroy it."

God decided to spare Lot and his family, but in doing so, there were instructions given.

Genesis 19:17

^{17} "As soon as they had brought them out, one of them said, "Flee for your lives! Don't look back, and don't stop anywhere in the plain! Flee to the mountains or you will be swept away!"

Lot's wife did not listen; she looked back after she had been told not to. Whatever the reason, she was disobedient, and it cost her life as she was turned into a pillar of *salt*.

Genesis 19:23-26

^{23} "By the time Lot reached Zoar, the sun had risen over the land. ^{24} Then the Lord rained down burning sulfur on Sodom and Gomorrah—from the Lord out of the heavens. ^{25} Thus he overthrew those cities and the entire plain, destroying all those living in the cities— and also the vegetation in the land. ^{26} But Lot's wife looked back, and she became a pillar of salt."

How many times has God delivered us from something and told us not to go back or look back to that very thing that He has delivered us from?

Looking back is the first step before you go back! There are always memories or feelings and emotions attached to whatever was in the past, whether good or bad.

Have you ever gone back to something that you know God made a way for you to get out the first time, and then it was ten times worse when you went back to it? Then the first thing out of our mouth is, "Lord, if you get me out of this thing, I will never go back." But why should He deliver us the next time around? We did not follow instructions the first time nor keep our promise to Him, for many of our lives depend on God's instructions, just as Lot's wife's life depended on God-given instructions. You see, God made a way of escape from destruction and tried to lead them to a new place, to give them a fresh start in their place of choice.

Unfortunately, by looking back, Lot's wife did not make it because whatever memories she carried in her thoughts caused her to look back.

Do not bring the Old to the New!

Lot's daughters brought the old to the new. God spared them. He showed grace and mercy because they were connected to Lot. They came from a wicked land where there were all sorts of evil and acts considered as an abomination unto God. The new land where they dwelled was in a cave. They were concerned because there were no men around for them to marry or have children with. They produced a plan to sleep with their father to have children.

Genesis 19:30-38

[31] "One day the older daughter said to the younger, "Our father is old, and there is no man around here to give us children—as is the custom all over the earth. [32] Let's get our father to drink wine and then sleep with him and preserve our family line through our father." [33] That night they got their father to drink wine, and the older daughter went in and

slept with him. He was not aware of it when she lay down or when she got up." ³⁴ *"The next day the older daughter said to the younger, "Last night I slept with my father. Let's get him to drink wine again tonight, and you go in and sleep with him so we can preserve our family line through our father."* ³⁵ *So they got their father to drink wine that night also, and the younger daughter went in and slept with him. Again he was not aware of it when she lay down or when she got up."* ³⁶ *" So both of Lot's daughters became pregnant by their father.* ³⁷ *The older daughter had a son, and she named him Moab[g]; he is the father of the Moabites of today.* ³⁸ *The younger daughter also had a son, and she named him Ben-Ammi[h]; he is the father of the Ammonites[i] of today."*

How many times have we looked at a situation, and because it seemed hopeless, we took things into our own hands instead of patiently waiting for God to provide? They resorted to the same wicked acts just as if they were still in Sodom and Gomorrah. They brought that same immorality into their "New" place, the place of new beginnings.

We know we will not literally turn into a pillar of salt, but we can say by Lot's wife turning into a pillar of salt that she died. She turned into a pillar of salt because she disobeyed God's instruction. The instructions were to go forward and get out of that place of sin, destruction, and immorality and not look back. Our emotional attachment to the things in our past can turn our goals, dreams, and aspirations into a pillar of salt if we allow it to consume us.

Many emotions from our past can bring up feelings that can hinder us from moving forward in life. We need to learn from our past but not live in it.

Luke 9:62: "And Jesus said unto him, No man, having put his hand to the plough, and looking back, is fit for the kingdom of God."

One of the emotions that can follow us from the past is fear. Fear can immobilize us and prevent us from moving forward. We may fear failing, being rejected, progressing or regressing, and so on. These are some of the feelings that fear can trigger. Fear does not come from God, as 2 Timothy 1:7 states, "For God hath not given us the spirit of fear; but of power, and of love, and of a sound mind." Since God did not give us the spirit of fear, we should renounce it and return it to where it belongs.

Fight! Your life depends on it!

In this book, "Stronger, Better, Wiser: Walk Into the New You," we encourage you to fight for your future. The battles of our minds are one of the biggest battles we must face, especially when we have chosen to live our lives on a path of righteousness, a life pleasing to God. The enemy tries to use tactics of our past to paralyze us. To make us feel unworthy and that our lives have not changed. He tries to make it seem like there is no growth and often tries to tell us we will never be anything, but we are here to tell you that is not so! Your life depends on your fight!

You have come too far to go backward or stay stuck in a time warp that has a chokehold over you. If you do so, you can stunt your progress. Be free today! God has more in store for us. You have not even fully tapped into the fullness of everything God has for you.

Deuteronomy 31:6

Be strong and of a good courage, fear not, nor be afraid of them: for the LORD thy God, he it is that doth go with thee; he will not fail thee, nor forsake thee.

Genesis 28:15 Look,

I am with you, and I will watch over you wherever you go, and I will bring you back to this land. For I will not leave you until I have done what I have promised you."

God promised us in His word that He will never leave or forsake us. Yes, along the way, there will be trials and tribulations. He will be with us in the fire. He never promised that we would not go through anything, but He promised to be there with us through it all, just like with the Hebrew boys Shadrach, Meshach, and Abednego (Daniel 3:8- 30). They were thrown into the fire because they refused to bow down to the king's golden image. They took a stand before God. There were supposed to be only three men in that fire, but scripture points out that there was a fourth man in the fire with them. The Hebrew boys still had to go through the test, but God stepped in with them and they walked out of the fire, not smelling like smoke. Not a hair was singed, nor were their clothes burned. God got into the situation with them, protected them, and delivered them out of their situation. Let this encourage you to know that no matter what you are going through, God is there protecting and covering you.

Daniel 3:27

And the princes, governors, and captains, and the king's counselors, being gathered together, saw these men, upon whose bodies the fire had no power, nor was a hair of their head singed, neither were their coats changed, nor the smell of fire had passed on them.

It is natural to go down memory lane from time to time. We are all human, and this happens, but the key is not to stay there long enough for it to do its damage. I now know that I have a full life ahead of me, and I know that you do too. I want to see all the good things that God has in store for me! There was a time in my life when I was not confident enough to say this. Life seemed to have been doing its thing, and I was letting it. But as time passes, God is teaching me not to just lie down and take anything that life throws at me. He is teaching me that I have control over my life and that He has given me the power to withstand and endure. He constantly reminds me to use the tools He gave me to fight.

When we fight, we are not necessarily fighting with our hands or weapons, but we are fighting in the spirit using the tools God has placed in us and in His word.

2 Corinthians 10:4

(For the weapons of our warfare are not carnal, but mighty through God to the pulling down of strong holds;).

Ephesians 6:12

For we wrestle not against flesh and blood, but against principalities, against powers, against the rulers of the darkness of this world, against spiritual wickedness in high places.

We can only engage in spiritual warfare if we are equipped with the armor of God, which consists of the following pieces: the belt of truth, which helps us to remain faithful to God's word and resist deception; the breastplate of righteousness, which protects our hearts and shields us from condemnation; the shoes of the gospel of peace, which enable us to walk in peace and share the good news with others; the shield of faith, which extinguishes the fiery darts of doubt and fear; and finally, the helmet of salvation, which secures our minds and assures us of our eternal destiny. To use the armor of God, we need to pray in the Spirit and wield the sword of the Spirit, which is the Word of God. The Word of God is our most powerful weapon against the enemy, who tries to accuse us, lie to us, and discourage us. When he brings up our past failures and makes us feel guilty, we can use the Word of God to remind him of his future doom. He always tries to make us lose hope and question God's love and forgiveness, so why not remind him of his judgment?

Matthew 25:41

Then He will say to those on His left, **'Depart from Me, you who are cursed***, into the eternal fire prepared for the devil and his angels.*

Remind him that in God, you are a new creation. Remind him that the old has passed away, even if it does not seem like it. Have faith that whatever God started in you, He will finish it. We all have a process, and some of our processes are faster in some areas than others, but that is okay. Keep moving forward, and you will eventually start seeing the change. You may start seeing that when people mention your past, you do not cry as much or get angry as fast as you used to. No matter how small the change is, it is still progress! Small wins eventually turn into big wins. Never compare someone else's progress to yours. You are unique, an original design, and each design has a different pattern to follow, but what matters is that you complete what you started, which is to be the best version of the "New You."

Simone Williams-Young

Simone Williams-Young can be described as a Dream and Vision encourager. She is a book publisher, entrepreneur, prophet, mentor, author, wife, grandmother, and, most importantly, a servant of the Most High God. Her goal is to inspire people to reach toward everything that God has in store for them. She believes that no matter what happened in the past, as long as God allows us to see a new day, there is always a chance to do better and be better.

Simone Williams-Young is the CEO and founder of Young at Heart Publishing LLC, which was birthed to empower individuals with a voice and a story to share with the world. Young at Heart LLC. provides every opportunity to accomplish their dreams. Simone Williams- Young is not only a successful author but also a mentor for aspiring writers. She has helped many people turn their ideas into books, guiding them through the process of planning, drafting, and publishing. She offers coaching services for anyone who wants to learn how to write and publish their own books. Some of the books she has mentored include *"The Purpose Formula: Uncover Your Life's Mission and Live with Passion"* and *"The Power of Purpose: How Personal Growth Leads to Leadership"* by Reuben L. Young, *"The Path to Success: Unlocking Your Mind's Full Potential"* by James Hewitt, and *"Breakdown to Breakthrough"* by Brenda J. Williams. Simone has worked on diverse types of writing projects, ranging from fiction to non-fiction, sci-fi to romance, Christian fiction, and more.

She is excited to share more of her work with you through Young at Heart Publishing LLC. Stay tuned for some amazing releases coming soon.

Simone Williams-Young is a woman of many talents and passions. She is the owner and founder of She Uniq LLC, a hair boutique that offers various services and products to enhance the beauty and uniqueness of women around the world. She believes that women have different ways and forms of expressing their beauty and wants to help them achieve their goals.

She is also the author of a book titled *"I Choose to Live: Pushing Through the Grieving Process."* This book is a personal testimony of how she overcame the loss of her son, who was killed in his prime by gun violence. She authored this book to inspire and empower others who are going through grief and to show them that they can survive and thrive. She also mentors and coaches other grieving individuals who need support and guidance to move forward.

Simone Williams-Young has been featured on Daughter of the King Television Network several times, and she is a board member of Heart 2 Heart Ministries International Foundation Non-Profit, a charitable organization led by Dr. Angela Roberson. She participates in various projects and initiatives that aim to help the community and spread the love of God.

Simone Williams-Young is a faithful member of Wrecking Crew for Christ Holiness Church, where Chief Apostle Michael L. Rowles is the leader. She has learned much from his teachings and examples about leadership, service, holiness, and love. She strives to live a life that pleases God and blesses others.

Contact Information:

FB- Author Simone Williams-Young, Simone Williams

Email: contact@Yahpublishingllc.com

Website: linktr.ee/SimoneWilliamsYoung

Stronger Together

Dr. Angela Roberson

Two people are better than one!

When two people work together, they get more work done. If one person falls, the other person can reach out to help. Often, we try and do things by ourselves, which is okay, but think how much more can be accomplished if we pull together to reach a common goal. There is great strength in numbers.

Often, I look at how much I did on the motorcycle set building a social club, Heart 2 Heart Compton Social Club, with women who were broken and who had no clue of their identity, women who did not have a relationship with God, women who were out just for the life of the party. Even in that, we were able to build and make an impact in a place that had no meaning to the purpose of God in our lives. I did not know who I was in God at that time; I just had influence. I knew how to gather. I knew how to put things together, and people would show up just for the party, drinking, sex, and so much more! But it was simply because we were on one accord and we did things together in unity.

Genesis 11:5-6:

And the LORD came down to see the city and the tower, which the children of man had built. And the LORD said, "Behold, they are one people, and they have all one language, and this is only the beginning of what they will do.

Biblically, it is important for us to work together in unity; then, we will understand what Ephesians 4:11 was talking about. Now, these are the gifts Christ gave to the church: the apostles, the prophets, the evangelists, and the pastors and teachers.

Paul underscores these four gifts in verses 11 and 12: *"His gifts were that some should be apostles, some prophets, some evangelists, some pastors and teachers, for the equipment of the saints, for the work of ministry, for building up of the body of Christ."*

Even when we go back and look at the day of Pentecost, when they were all in one room, one place, and they were able to see signs, wonders, and miracles, even in other languages, how powerful is it to see so many things in the capacity of two?

Acts 2:2 NIV

"When the day of Pentecost came, they were all together in one place. Suddenly a sound like the blowing of a violent wind came from heaven and filled the whole house where they were sitting. They saw what seemed to be tongues of fire that separated and came to rest on each of them."

Esther demonstrated exceptional bravery and strength, willing to fulfill God's purpose for her life, whatever the cost. While she could have been killed for visiting the king unannounced, she knew that a cause greater than herself was at stake. The story of Esther emphasizes the power of God, instructing us to use the blessings given by God to help others. For children, the moral of the story of Esther is to always do the right thing, using the influence you possess. When I read the story of Esther, it shows the power of unity and how strong we can be working together as she did with her uncle Mordecai and the rest of the people!

THE ESTHER ANOINTING

Becoming a woman of prayer, courage, and influence gives you the keys to Esther's success. God gave you the power of influence and the key to finding God's favor for your assignment. God can use your life for His glory, no matter where you come from or your skills and talents. The fact that Esther was able to navigate the complicated politics of the palace and even got the king to kill his grand vizier shows her wisdom and intelligence. She knows how to use whatever little right she has to her own advantage, something that her Uncle Mordecai taught her, and she learned how to become one of the greatest collaborators ever known in her time. Queen Esther acted courageously when she decided to gather Shushan's Jews, fast, and approach the king. She had the courage to plan the feasts and the timing to make her requests. She further had the courage to beg King Ahasuerus to save the Jews after Haman's demise and made further requests. Courage breeds courage. In the history of Christianity, Esther is not only a queen but a liberator. She did not force her power on anyone.

Her sacrificial love for her people makes her stand out as someone who used her power for good. Her impressive wisdom and ingenuity gave her a seat beside all other great women in history. She prayed to the Lord God of Israel and said: "O my Lord, you only are our king; help me, who am alone and have no helper but you, for my danger is in my hand." When people unite and work together, they can achieve great things. As the saying goes, 'When two or more agree on something, it shall be established, and they shall see the manifestation of it.' I'm reminded of Esther's story and how her call was a testament to this principle. She asked her maidens and the Jews in the land to fast with her. After three days of fasting, she went to the king and obtained favor in his sight. Some of the greatest things we will learn in the Book of Esther are how to do things together and how much stronger we are when we are in unity and one accord.

In this Bible story, we will learn from a man named Mordecai in the Book of Esther. We will learn from his example of caring for others, doing the right thing no matter what, and remaining faithful to God. We will learn that we should never grow tired of doing the right thing. Looking at Esther's story, I see myself so much in this story when I think about all of the times that I've had to fast and call for unity in the fast so that I can defeat the enemy that continuously rises against me, trying to hinder what God has for me. Esther is a prime example of how the enemy kept trying to take her and her people out! We are stronger together. "Go, gather all the Jews who are in Susa, and fast for me. Do not eat or drink for three days, night or day. I and my maids will fast as you do. When this is done, I will go to the king, even though it is against the law." When I look at the servant heart of this woman and how she was willing to sacrifice her own life for the one she loved, what better person could you have on your side willing to fight for you, even if it takes their life? Cultivate a servant heart. Esther's servant heart shines through in many ways. Her obedience to God in answering His call, her devotion to Mordecai, her humble service to the king, and her willingness to sacrifice it all for her people establish her as a woman of God who puts others before herself.

In this section, I reflect on three ways in which, if you read Esther 4, it can speak to believers in a crisis. Firstly, it speaks of the role of lament, which is to mourn. Secondly, it highlights the importance of seeking God's help through prayer and fasting. Finally, it reminds us that times of crisis call for solidarity, which is unity. After all that, Esther takes on the mission of her life, only after ensuring that the people are united behind her: "Go and gather all the Jews… and fast for my sake... for three days, night and day; Then I will go to the king…" (**Book of Esther 4:16**). Will we learn that lesson today? The story of Esther emphasizes the power of God, instructing us to use the blessings given by Him to help others. Again, I say that two are better than one; we are stronger together if only one day, we get how good and pleasing it is for brothers to dwell together in unity (Psalm 133 A song of ascents. Of David). How good and pleasant it is when brothers live together in unity! It is like precious oil poured on the head, running down on the beard, running down on Aaron's.

Even when I look back over when I had Monday night prayers at my house in Compton from 2013 through 2014, I see that they were powerful. We saw signs, wonders, and miracles happening almost every Monday. We would spend hours in prayer; three, five, eight hours in prayer! I remember this one particular night we were having prayer, and my oldest son was sitting on the couch. We were walking back and forth, just praying, talking to the Lord, and all of a sudden, I heard the Holy Spirit say, "I'm about to fill your son," and soon as I turned and walked towards him, he just began to speak in tongues. He was filled with the Holy Ghost sitting right there on the couch. Nobody had to lay hands on him. Nobody had to touch him. The Holy Spirit did it all by itself.

Oftentimes, I would wonder as I go to different churches throughout my ministry and see people literally slapping people around just for them to receive the Holy Ghost. When I got filled with the Holy Ghost, I was at a lake, walking down to the water doing a prayer, and before I knew it, I began to speak in another language that I knew nothing of. I became afraid because I was not sure what was happening to me. So see, here is a prime example that when you want the Holy Ghost to come in, He knows when your heart is ready to receive Him. At that time, I was desperate for what God wanted to do in my life. A prophet had told me that God was calling me to him, and it was time for me to answer. God had to do quick work in me to prepare me for the purpose, plan, and great commission for what He had called me to do. It was time for me to get my life in order. I had been chucking and jiving for much too long, and God was saying, "Receive me now or lose your life forever." I did not know I had such a great calling on my life. I did not know that God would send me to Africa, Jamaica, Mexico, and other places to do my ministry.

I look back on that time right before being converted, when I was on the motorcycle set, just coming out of a divorce from an 18-year relationship. I was just out there doing what I thought was best to keep me from losing my mind. See, that is how the enemy can fool you if you do not have anyone to talk to you. Yeah, I had people I could talk to, but they were leading me the wrong way. But once God sent His prophet to speak to me, everything changed in my life. All the things I had gone through, the things that God had even allowed me to learn, He used it for my ministry. God gets the glory out of your life even when you do not live the right life. Sadly, I was doing all the wrong things, thinking it was for all the right reasons. However, that's where we make our biggest mistakes—when we don't seek godly counsel and instead turn to man's advice. If we take the time to allow the Holy Ghost to connect us with the right people at the right time, in the right place, in the right season of our lives, we will never fail. We will always be blessed because it's not about us; it's about God and the divine purpose for our lives.

Even looking back over my life, when I didn't even know the Bible, I see that God had placed a good friend and apostle in my life to help me learn the Word of God. I would wake up at 2 AM, and God would give me a scripture that I'd never heard before. I would call her on the phone, tell her what I heard, and she would have me go to the scripture and read it to her. Every time we did something together, we witnessed signs, wonders, and miracles.

That's why I know the significance of working together with someone who is in one accord with you, just as the Bible talks about: "How can we work together unless we agree? How do two walk together unless they have agreed to do so?" (**Amos 3:3**).

This thought-provoking Biblical quote emphasizes the importance of agreement for effective collaboration and companionship. Examples abound of why unity is crucial, not only in the workplace, where it fosters productivity and happiness among employees striving toward a common goal, but also biblically, where unity is highlighted as essential.

"Two is better than one!" I remember meeting two prayer warriors from Africa who knew some of my history from Africa. They decided to be prayer partners for me until God released them from the assignment. Every day, they sent me prayers and scriptures during some of the toughest times in my life dealing with a warlock from Africa. I survived. He said I would be dead before 2014, but it is now 2023, and God kept me. I am here solely by the grace of God; prayer saved my life. Unity with prayer warriors covering me on every side. Stronger together, I truly believe, because it's a different force of power that combines itself to overthrow anything that is not aligned with God. He has already said, "How good and pleasing is it for brethren, to dwell gathering unity" **Psalms 133:1.** We have to understand that this was God's plan all along. Two is better than one.

Dr. Angela Roberson

The prophet Angela Roberson is known as an Apostle of Prayer. She is a native of California and a mother of 3 sons: Brian Hilt, Mark Carter, and Angelo Carter. Apostle is an entrepreneur, a global speaker, the C.E.O and Founder of Heart 2 Heart Ministries International Foundation Non-Profit, Heart 2 Heart Food Pantry, Heart 2 Heart Multi-Purpose Center, and the CEO of True Kingdom Records. She is also the television host of "Prayer Saved My Life." By the grace of God, she is now the founder of her own television network "Daughter of the King TV Network." Angela has her bachelor's degree in biblical studies and counseling. A push from several great leaders with Godly mentoring and counseling led Apostle Roberson to the ministry of prayer and deliverance, where she established her initial center to serve God's people. Heart 2 Heart Ministry International Foundation was birthed in Ghana, Africa, and led her to other countries: Jamaica, Mexico, and the Bahamas. Apostle Roberson also founded an all-girls school in Pakistan. She has no regrets in answering the call of God. However, by no means has it been easy raising 3 sons, preaching, teaching, mentoring, and traveling to different states and countries. Angela Roberson always finds time to pour into others and is a woman of prayer, passion, and integrity. She often says that she cannot do this without the presence and the power of God.

MY JOURNEY:

ARF Administration Development Disabled Adults acquired in 2007: Worked for Alondra Homes with level 4I clients between the years 2008-2009. Also worked with other source of clients, including but not limited to the mentally ill, artistic, and disadvantaged children.

Cardiac Technician License acquired in 1993:

Began working for L.A. County in 2000 as a Cardiac Technician in the Emergency Room at Harbor UCLA Medical Center.

Retired early in 2016.

Apostle Angela Roberson completed all of the requirements for elevation to the office of Apostle in the Gospel of Jesus Christ in June 2014

The Church of the Scattered Flock Intl. Archbishop Anna R Neal.

In 2016, she received the Humanitarian Award under the Ministerial Alliance at City of Refuge, under the leadership of Bishop Noel Jones.

In 2016-now, she was a host of Prayer Saved My Life on the Cross TV Network.

In 2017, she earned her bachelor's degree in biblical studies and counseling at Bible Believers College Seminary, graduating cum laude.

In 2017, she received the Award for Prayer at Bible Believers College Seminary.

From 2017-2019, she worked as a PR for Cross TV Network

In 2018, she received the Award of Appreciation under the Ministerial Alliance at City of Refuge.

In 2021, she was awarded appreciation for Outstanding Support to Passion to Love and Care Ministries, under the leadership of CEO Founder Prophetess Temika McCanns.

However, her success does not stop there. Apostle Roberson has been the guest speaker on different local radio and international TV stations such as The Cross-TV Network, OCN Broadcasting, KGLH Radio Station, Motherland Show, and K-Day FM Radio Station. She is also the author of *The Path of My Deliverance and Full Fledge: Understanding the Power of Faith*. She has also been featured in Pastor S.L. Maxwell-Robles Magazine.

As impressive as Apostle Roberson's accolades sound, her love for God and His people is her drive and the focus of everything that she puts her hands to do. She is a firm believer that promotion ONLY comes from God (Psalm 75:6-7).

Executing Wisdom Destroys the Foolishness in Life

Brenda J. Williams

Crazy is doing the same thing and expecting different results! The old people used to say, "A hard head makes a soft behind." In other words, you can welcome the Wisdom of God and instructions that produce the answers we need or fail to listen and fall into the snares, traps, heartaches, and pains of life.

When we find out that our life is surrounded by chaos, confusion, and drama all the time, we must ask ourselves what we are doing wrong and identify the source. We need to find out what the people that surround us are about! Today, you cannot let everybody into your life. You have associates and friends. We need to distinguish what category and status to give people. You must do research on people, ask questions, and find out who people really are. It is important to know who is in your close circle and around you.

If you are getting married, you may even need to do a background check, seek marriage counseling, pray, fast, and ask God to expose the heart of the person you want to marry. Ask God to give you wisdom and His keen discernment about the person and others in your life. "God, reveal and expose anything hidden! God, shine the light on any evil, darkness, abusive spirits, or mental illness." Unfortunately, people are not who they appear to be these days! Everyone that smiles in your face is not for you! Some people want what you have, or they want to tap into the success that you have worked and earned. Some may want to be you! Some people are sent on assignment to purposefully cause evil, chaos, and destruction in your life. They just do not like you! Some people have hidden agendas and motives! Some people are good and genuine people! This also goes for going into business with people and making important business moves. You just do not know, so you must pray and ask God to show you who people really are. Boundaries must be set with people! We need to find out what type of god people serve and what they believe in, because what people believe in will influence your decision, especially if they are close to you. A person's life experiences, habits, and thoughts, whether good or bad, can spill over into your life by association. Wrong doors can be opened by operating with the wrong people! We must choose wisely who speaks into our lives. This is why we have the Holy Bible, "The Word of God," to study, to give us Godly wisdom to help us navigate through life. The Bible says in 2 Timothy 2:15:

> *Study to show thyself approved unto God, a workman that needeth not to be ashamed, rightly dividing the Word of God.*

The Bible also says in James 1:5:

> *If any of you lack wisdom, let him ask of God, that giveth to all men liberally and upbraideth not, and It shall be given him.*

If we do not read or study the Word of God, we will not know the Word of God, nor will we have a measuring stick or barometer to judge from right and wrong. When we need wisdom, we must come to God and ask Him to give us His wisdom on every situation and problem that may be in our lives. God says that He gives us wisdom liberally, meaning that God does not withhold wisdom but willingly and freely gives us all the wisdom we need just for the asking.

As believers, we do not go to palm readers, play Ouija Boards, or go to tarot card readers. This is unspiritual and demonic counsel!

We have the Holy Spirit, who leads and guides us into all truth. We must seek Godly wisdom from the Holy Bible. We must seek Godly counselors who teach from the Word of God. The Holy Bible is the only true source of God's Word. The Bible says in Proverbs 11:14:

Where no counsel is the people fall:
But in the multitude of counselors there is safety

We want to be led by the "Spirit of God" in everything we do. Human wisdom is earthly and unspiritual knowledge validated through science and life experiences. Divine wisdom originates from the ultimate source of all wisdom, understanding, and counsel through the Holy Spirit. We need to seek and ask God for the Wisdom of God based on the Word of God. The Bible says in Hosea 4:6:

My people are destroyed for a lack of knowledge; because you have rejected knowledge, I will also reject thee, that thou shall be no more priest to me. In all thy ways acknowledge Him, and he will direct our paths path. [Proverbs 3:6]

We must read and study God's Word to gain knowledge and understanding to make the right decisions in life. If you listen to earthly counsel and earthly knowledge, you are not guaranteed results, but God's Wisdom and His Word always guarantee results and keep us from making mistakes.

We need to apply and execute wisdom that destroys the foolishness that would try to enter our lives.

The Bible says in Matthew 24:35:

Heaven and earth shall pass away but my words shall not pass away.

The Word of God is sharper than a two-edged Sword piercing even to the dividing asunder of soul and spirit, and of the joints and marrow, and is a discerner of the thoughts and Intents of the heart.
[Hebrews 4:12]

You can depend on the "Word of God" to bring you out of every circumstance. We must speak and declare God's Word over our circumstances to get results. If we do not stand on the Word of God in our situations, we will find ourselves not getting our prayers answered and not obtaining victory. The devil knows where you stand in your faith, and he will keep bringing havoc in your life.

God delivered the children of Israel out of Egypt through Moses. The children of Israel wandered in the wilderness for 40 years in the Book of Exodus. In the wilderness, they had to walk through the desert on their journey. There were a few camels, but overall, every person individually did not have one. The desert was a hot and dry place! They were tired of being in the wilderness, so they allowed their bad attitude to surface with fear and disobedience. Instead of trusting God and using their faith, they started murmuring and complaining against Moses and missed going into the "Promised Land." God allowed all the elderly to die off in the wilderness. God hates disobedience, murmuring, and complaining, especially against His anointed servants.

Often, when you are going through hardship and are experiencing a "wilderness experience" in your life, you must not allow yourself to begin to murmur and complain instead of trusting God's Word to deliver you. The children of Israel had no lamp posts along the roads at night; it was pitch black except for the fire in the sky. They had run out of food and were hungry, but whenever Moses would pray, God provided water and food for them in the desert. God had provided everything they needed with miracles, signs, and wonders, and they still did not trust God, murmuring and complaining.

Moses did not have a GPS, nor did they have cell phones back then. The children of Israel were led by the clouds by day and the pillar of fire at night. God was with them! The pillar of fire and the clouds represented God's power and that God was with them to protect them. If the Children of Israel had believed and trusted in

God and took God at His Word, it would not have taken them 40 years to get to the Promised Land. They would have reached their destination sooner!

A "wilderness season" can be a dry place of hardship and sorrow! It can seem like God is not with you and is not listening! It can also feel like you have been thrown in the fire like Shadrach, Meshach, and Abednego mentioned in Daniel Chapter 1:19. A "wilderness season" can be of great hardship, suffering, and pain. It can feel like the lions are about to eat you up! The devil is there to trick you into believing that God is not with you and to convince you that you are not coming out. You must walk by the Word of God by faith and not by what you see in the natural. You must meditate, believe, and read the Word of God, get the Word down in your heart, and confess the Word of God with power against the circumstances until the circumstances change. Suffering and hardship can also draw us into an intimate relationship with God. If we have not been praying, the fiery trials and tribulations push us to pray where God now has our attention. God can teach you now and show you how to fight with the Word of God and bring you out. You may think you are going under; you may think you are going to be swallowed up, but God is with you to deliver you. When you pray, the Holy Spirit will comfort you and give you directions, divine strategies, and divine solutions to bring you out of your trial or "wilderness season" with victory if you listen! God said in His Word in Hebrews 13:5:

...God has said, "I will never leave you or forsake you."

God determines how long you will stay in your "wilderness season."

There are lessons you must learn! We start out as babies in the faith, and then we develop into stronger, mature children of God who know how to stand on the Word of God no matter what the situation is and fight back with the Word. You will become confident and know that God will bring you out! You will stand firm, knowing that this too shall pass! You will learn that God delivers you out of everything the devil will throw at you. You will then know how to help others stand tall in their trials and "wilderness seasons." You can then teach others how to fight spiritually and win. This is when the devil hates that you get up in the morning! You have been tested and proven! He knows you are armed and dangerous with the Word of God.

How you hear God and how quickly you do it God's way will determine how fast you come out of your "wilderness season." The Holy Spirit is your GPS navigator, and He will lead and guide you into all truth. The Holy Spirit is your light in the darkness! The Holy Spirit will show you the way out! God will even send people to you to confirm what the Holy Spirit has spoken to you. We can receive the way out through the Holy Spirit's instructions or choose to do it our own way with our natural mind and stay in the trial for a long time.

Remember, the trial is for a season and has an expiration date! The trial is not going to last forever! You either pass the test or not. If you do not pass, you may have to start all over with another test. We want to get the test right the first time if we can, but this does not always happen. We all must learn at our own pace and with our own faith. Each one of us learns differently and processes differently. God loves us and trains us each individually. Our faith and trust in God is developed through the experiences we go through. God knows when to end your "wilderness experience." He knows what He wants to get out of your life and what He is doing. God knows what will make you stronger, better, and wiser. We must put all our trust in God. God sees the big picture of our entire life; we do not! There is an old saying, "It may not feel good to you, but it is good for you."

One major determining factor in our trials is obedience. God said in Isaiah 1:19:

If ye be willing and obedient, ye shall eat the good of the Land.

When we are obedient to God's Word, it plays an important role in the tests and tribulations we go through. God put His power of the Holy Spirit inside of us. God will do miracles for you as you stand, believe, and confess the Word of God and watch God move on your behalf. God will provide for you in your "wilderness season." God will honor His Word.

The children of Israel saw God perform miracles after miracles right before their very eyes through Moses and still doubted that God would take care of them. They allowed their fear to become louder than what God was telling them and doing for them. The opposite of faith is fear. Their fears took them right out of faith, and they did not trust God. The devil will always use someone or something to steer you off course. Fear consists of the wrong thoughts and imaginations that will take you further away from your victory and leave you wide open to being defeated. You do not want to have to repeat your test! You do not want to be like the children of Israel and doubt God and His power to deliver you. You want to get it right the first time. You want to keep the Word of God before you and in your heart. Be obedient and follow God's instructions. The Bible says in Deuteronomy 3:18:

The Lord himself goes before you and will be with You; he will never leave you nor forsake you. Do not be Afraid; do not be discouraged.

The Bible says in John 10:10:

The thief (the devil) cometh not, but for to steal, and to kill, and to destroy: I am come that they might have life, and that they might have it more abundantly.

God called the children of Israel to come to Him through the desert. God knew that it was not going to be easy, but He was with them to fight for them. We must trust God in our "wilderness season" that God is going to bring us out. You cannot let fear come in and make you afraid. You must build your faith by confessing scriptures of God's faithfulness to you from the Word of God.

Some think that when we get saved, we are not supposed to get sick and experience any difficulties in life. This is far from the truth! Jesus had to go to the cross so we could have eternal life. Jesus was beaten, pierced in His side, stripped naked, and humiliated on the cross. We will go through challenging times also. What we are going through may be painful, but have faith in God. If God brought you to it, God will bring you through it! You are coming out Stronger, Better, and Wiser! You are getting ready to walk in the "New You" with better wisdom, insight, authority, and power. The Bible says in Hebrews 5:8-1:

Though he were a Son, yet learned he obedience by the things which he suffered; and being made perfect, he became the author of eternal salvation unto all them that **obey** *him;*

The "wilderness season" is not easy or comfortable, but it is necessary and beneficial for our spiritual growth and maturity. It is a time of testing and training, pruning and refining, dying and rising, losing and gaining. It is a time of transformation and renewal, revelation and encounter, promise and fulfillment. It is a time of grace and glory, of faith and hope, of love and joy. It is a time of wilderness and wonder. God does the miraculous when you trust Him.

The children of Israel wanted to do things their way and, through their disobedience, ended up missing the Promised Land. We do not want to be disobedient and miss what God has for us. How we manage our life situations will determine how fast we come out of our "wilderness season" and enter our "victory season" or our "Promised Land." God wants you to win! God wants you to overcome, but you must be obedient to the Word of God and do things God's way or suffer the consequences.

Let us look at the parable of the ten virgins! Five of the virgins were wise, and five of the virgins were foolish! Let us look at how these foolish virgins managed the instructions given to them. The Bible says in Matthew 25:1-13,

"Then shall the kingdom of heaven be likened unto ten virgins who took their lamps and went forth to meet the bridegroom, and five of them were wise, and five were foolish."

This scripture shows that the ten virgins were given the opportunity to use wisdom or walk in foolishness with their decisions. The ten virgins were going to meet the bridegroom (Jesus), but the wise virgins read the manual, got instructions on their trip to meet Jesus, and prepared themselves. The wise virgins were not going on their trip blind, dumb, and stupid! The wise virgins had checked how many miles they were going to cover, confirmed how much oil they would need in their lanterns, and purchased wicks for their lanterns.

Lanterns with wicks are devices that produce light by burning oil or other fuels. The wick is a piece of cloth or fiber that absorbs the fuel and carries it to the flame. The flame heats up the fuel and vaporizes it, creating a bright and steady light. Lanterns with wicks can be made of metal, glass, or ceramic and have different shapes and designs. Oil lanterns use lamp oil or kerosene as fuel. They have a metal burner that holds the wick and a glass chimney that protects the flame from wind and dust. Oil lanterns can be adjusted by changing the length of the wick or the amount of air that reaches the flame.

So, the five wise virgins were packed and ready to meet Jesus. They did their homework and counted the cost of their journey to meet Jesus. If you ask me, they had to be the first Girl Scouts in the land! They were packed and ready to go.

Now, the five foolish virgins were just galloping through life, not learning from life experiences, most likely busybodies, and not seeking the wisdom from their elders that they needed for their journey. They went to visit everybody in the village, chatting and unprepared.

These five virgins started their journey to meet Jesus with just their lamps and a little bit of oil. It took a long time for the bridegroom to come and meet them, so all the virgins fell asleep. At midnight, the cry rang out, "The bridegroom is come, come ye out to meet him." Well, all the virgins woke up when they heard the cry to come and meet the bridegroom for the wedding. The wise virgins had filled and trimmed their lamps with oil, were focused, and went straight away to meet Jesus.

The five foolish virgins had not prepared themselves for the journey. They had not bought any extra oil to trim their lamps. They were like most people when they had not done their homework or were not prepared for the things of life; they would want to borrow and take from you. They would want to take your hard-earned money or whatever you have obtained in life. They are called leeches, but they are going to learn today! So, the five foolish virgins tried to tip up to the wise virgins and ask them for some of their oil. The wise virgins simply told them they were not giving them any of their extra oil, so they should go buy their own oil, that if they gave them some of their oil, they would not have enough for themselves.

While the five foolish virgins had to go and try and find some oil, the bridegroom came, who was Jesus, and the five wise virgins went with Jesus to the wedding. The five foolish virgins found the five wise virgins and tried to get in at the wedding. They called out to Jesus, screaming and asking Jesus to let them in, but the door shut. Jesus said to the five virgins, "I do not know you!" Now you know that hurt. Look what foolishness and disobedience got them by not being prepared! They missed going to the wedding with Jesus! Excuses will not work with God! When we are disobedient to God, we bring upon ourselves unnecessary pain and suffering, sometimes even death! The five foolish virgins missed Jesus!

What an awful place to be!

We want to get it right when God gives us instructions. We must watch and pray because we do not know the day or the hour when Jesus will return for us. We do not want to be caught up in any foolishness like the five foolish virgins and miss God. We will not be able to ride on anybody else's coat tail. Let us be diligent and vigilant about the things of God. Let us read, meditate, pray, and stay in good fellowship with God so we can have good success in our lives. We saw earlier how the children of Israel did not listen to God; they murmured and complained and were disobedient and wandered in the wilderness for 40 years. They were invited to enter the "Promised Land" flowing with milk and honey but missed God through their disobedience.

Many of us know better but will not do better! Sometimes, we think that God is going to just keep winking at our ignorance. Not so! It is by our obedience and keeping the Word of God in our lives that we are blessed by God.

When you study and read the Word of God, then you have obtained Godly wisdom and knowledge on an issue. Only then can you execute the wisdom you have learned from the Word of God and eradicate foolishness from your life. God has left His manual, which is the Holy Bible. Now, it is your time to pick it up, use it, and line yourself up with the Word of God.

I pray that God will be your strength and lead and guide you through every circumstance of life with His wisdom and understanding. I pray that God will show you every trap of the enemy ahead of time so you can eradicate it. I pray that God covers you in the blood of Jesus and protects you.

I decree and declare that you will win in every area of your life in the New Year. I decree and declare that no weapon formed against you shall prosper, and every tongue which rises against you in judgment shall condemn. "'This is the heritage of the Servants of the Lord, and their righteousness is from Me,' says the Lord." I pray that God gives you a hunger and a thirst for His Word and that you will succeed and do things differently. We are going to be Better, Stronger, and Wiser in the New Year in Jesus' Name! Amen!

Brenda J. Williams

Brenda J. Williams is the author of "Breakdown to Breakthrough." Brenda is also the CEO of Building Walls Community Improvement Corporation (BWCIC). BWCIC builds up the walls of hope in the community by bringing outreach programs, conferences, workshops, and stage plays through the performing arts and other media platforms to teach and include at-risk teens. Brenda is currently a playwright, producer, and director of her own stage play, "The Five Foolish Virgins." Brenda is currently a pastor under the leadership of Chief Apostle Michael L. Rowles at the Wrecking Crew for Christ Holiness Church in Los Angeles. Brenda is truly a "walking miracle" that God is a healer! Brenda began experiencing anxiety, depression, fear, and nervousness while going through a divorce. Brenda was on her way to a sanitarium, but God stepped in and healed her mind through prayer and applying the Word of God. This book is written to encourage, strengthen, and give the reader hope that God can restore their mind! "Breakdown to Breakthrough" informs, instructs, and teaches you how to cope with fear, anxiety, and depression through spiritual tools given through the Word of God. Author Brenda J. Williams is a living testimony that the Word of God works! Brenda J. Williams is available for speaking engagements, book readings, women's conferences, and retreats.

Contact Information:

FB: Author Brenda J. Williams
FB: The Play, "The Five Foolish Virgins"
Website: linktr.ee/BrendaJWilliams
Email: authorbrendajwilliams@gmail.com
brendawilliamsbwcic@gmail.com

The Power of Your Inner Strength

Reuben L. Young Sr.

Inner strength is a quality many people aspire to have, especially when they are faced with difficult situations and challenges. But what does it mean to have inner strength, and where does it come from?

According to the dictionary, inner strength is "the ability to cope well with difficulties or to face a demanding situation in a spirited and resilient way." It is also sometimes called fortitude, courage, endurance, perseverance, or resilience. These are all admirable qualities that can help us overcome obstacles and achieve our goals in life.

God's Word teaches us that inner strength is not something we can develop on our own but rather a gift from God. In fact, the Bible teaches us that our natural human strength is actually a weakness and that we need to rely on God's power and grace to overcome our limitations and challenges. Paul writes in 2 Corinthians 12:9-10:

"But he said to me, 'My grace is sufficient for you, for my power is made perfect in weakness.' Therefore I will boast all the more gladly about my weaknesses, so that Christ's power may rest on me. That is why, for

Christ's sake, I delight in weaknesses, in insults, in hardships, in persecutions, in difficulties. For when I am weak, then I am strong."

Paul understood that his inner strength was not based on his own abilities or achievements but on his relationship with God. He knew that God's grace was enough to sustain him in any situation and that God's power was at work in him when he faced opposition and suffering. He also knew that his weaknesses were not something to be ashamed of but opportunities to experience God's grace and power more fully.

This does not mean that Paul was passive or resigned to his circumstances. On the contrary, he was active and diligent in fulfilling his calling and spreading the gospel. He did not rely on his own strength or wisdom but on God's guidance and provision. He also did not let his challenges discourage him or make him bitter but rather rejoiced in them as a way of glorifying God and growing in faith.

Self-Reflection, Isolation, and Re-focus

Similar to Paul's experience, I had to take a deep look within myself and evaluate my weaknesses. I realized I should not be ashamed of them but instead use them to strengthen my relationship with God. I began to rely on His strength, power, and grace to make necessary changes within myself. This period of my life was marked by self-reflection, isolation, and re-focusing. When facing challenges in life, sometimes you have to isolate yourself to re-focus, which also means concentrating. This allows us to approach all issues from different angles, hopefully with a better view for clarity. This is literally what I had to do when facing many difficulties at hand with which I was challenged. The eyes in the mirror staring back at me were a reminder that I had previous victories under my belt when it came to dealing with my challenges. I had mentally defeated giants and boogiemen from childhood until my adult life (fighting my own demons), walking in the supernatural power of inner strength and endurance power. Doing this allowed me to attack my obstacle with confidence and faith, to know that I could get past this. The key was not to play the victim. In doing so, I learned that what was imparted to me were the tools I needed to conquer anything that I was up against. Sure, it was easy to sit back and throw a pity party or point the finger, as some of us may do sometimes. But I knew that I was in this place called unbearable circumstances for a reason. Re-focusing allowed me to know that I had what it took to endure the process, to know that I'm more than a conqueror.

Romans 8:37

*37 Nay, in all these things we are more
than conquerors through him that loved us.*

Identifying your qualities, strengths, and what you have to work with is most important in any situation because self-reflection helps identify what is beneath the surface. Of course, my own mind tried to tell me to give up, and of course, I actually considered listening to it. Now, I'm so glad that I didn't listen to that voice in my head. Feelings of being bagged into a corner or stuck in between a rock and a hard place forced me to take a stand. The issues of life had me against the ropes, but I could not lose hope in GOD or myself. Depression, stress, and anxiety tried to attack me from all angles with force, and I was surrounded by negativity and ignorance that I had to block it all out at any cost.

2 Cor 13: 5-7

⁵Examine yourselves to see whether you are in the faith; test yourselves. Do you not realize that Christ Jesus is in you—unless, of course, you fail the test? ⁶And I trust that you will discover that we have not failed the test. ⁷Now we pray to God that you will not do anything wrong—not so that people will see that we have stood the test but so that you will do what is right even though we may seem to have failed.

Consistently examining myself was essential to achieve the results I needed. Time management was another key factor I utilized while working on myself because I knew that giving up and staying down would only lead to being stuck. Refusing to succumb to such a fate, I held on to the belief that "if it does not kill you, it will only make you stronger." It wasn't just a cliché but a real-life truth for me. Recognizing that trials and tribulations were merely tests of my faith put me in a better position to continue fighting against whatever obstacles came my way. Counting my victories and blessings gave me the encouragement that I needed not to give up. Recognizing that I had a powerful desire to become better, stronger, and wiser because of the depths from which I was raised, I knew that this too shall pass. The fight I was in seemed too big to win, but I had to have the confidence and the trust that I could win. My strong desire to become a better me had to be solid and unwavering. Sometimes, when I did not receive immediate results, discouragement tried to settle in, so speaking to myself became a habit because my spirits were immediately uplifted every time I talked to myself.

It is so important to encourage yourself and speak about yourself positively.

Self-Denial, Self-Destruction, & Distraction

Upon conducting a thorough inventory and self-evaluation, I came to the realization that I had several personal issues that needed to be addressed. I had been in denial, refusing to acknowledge that I had any problems to work on. This denial was a harmful weapon that was holding me back from identifying the root of my issues. For many years, my refusal to confront my problems kept me from making progress in my life. Eventually, this self-denial led to self-destruction as I continued to avoid the difficult task of addressing my problems. Sometimes, I have a tendency to give reasons for my problems and dwell on them. Feelings of hurt, unforgiveness, bitterness, and mixed emotions motivated me to pretend everything was alright. But deep down inside, I knew that I needed to work on myself and become a better version of myself. Unfortunately, I didn't confront these issues, which led to self-destruction.

The worst damage is internal damage, hemorrhaging and internal bleeding, going unnoticed. As many of you know, it is so easy to become distracted with life in general that self-care easily goes unnoticed and becomes hard to address. This is where extreme focus comes into play: when you want to better yourself and desire to see a change and become stronger. You must first get the information you need to refocus and fight all the distractions that try to enter your mind.

For me, I needed discipline and self-control in my prayer life to fight distractions. I had to make sure I was consistent and committed to it because I was determined to see the better man that I knew that I could be. I knew I was good at something other than what I was doing, and I wanted to really see it and also live it. I was blessed to have examples around me just to show me that it was possible. I had a hope and a why pushing me to become greater. Consistent prayer and research gave me the information and tools that I needed to work with while I was slowly chipping away at old pieces of old ways, old behaviors, and old attitudes, and it helped me see a difference. I guess you can call it being chiseled into the best model of myself that I can be. You have to want it, and I believe that you can do it. "For greater is He that is in me than He that is in the world" is a scripture that I like to quote, and once I decided to quote that scripture myself, I started to believe it. The realization of being a work in progress and refusing to give up makes it hard to lose. When you are committed to something, being consistent has a tendency to become easy. I had to get serious about myself and wanting to be introduced to the better me, which was already on the inside. Re-educating yourself and investing in yourself helps transform the mindset of moving forward to a Stronger, Better, and Wiser experience. Your gifts and your overall skill set will allow you to rise to the next level. The battle is between the spiritual mindset, the natural mindset, and the carnal mindset. There is a wrestling match going on in your head while becoming more spiritually empowered. Prayer and consistency allowed me to gain an advantage over the former mindsets.

I had to rename things to look at it from a unique perspective. I have noticed that I have become more confident in myself as I have gotten older. Due to this, I have started making better choices and decisions for my life.

Instead of making decisions quickly, I take my time to think things through and meditate on them. This has helped me see the full scope of things and obtain information that has been helpful in operating with wisdom. By doing this, I have become stronger in my confidence, self-esteem, and overall character, continuously encouraging myself that I was on the right path to reinventing myself. I have come to realize it is not a certain level to reach quickly, but this seems to be a lifelong journey for me at this stage. My own mirror seems to remind me every time that I still have work to do internally. I am not satisfied but content and sure that I am still under construction. One of the many tools I have gravitated to use on myself has been the shovel, and as we know, the function of that shovel is to dig and remove. Constant prayer, fasting, studying the Bible, steady research, and reading or listening to other helpful material have really begun to shape and mold a different me. Avoiding negativity, doubt, fears, and self-destruction can be a difficult feat at times, but the best thing is not to give in and not give up on yourself. Prayer is the catalyst that builds power for you to be able to manage your behavior.

GOD gave us the power, tools, gifts, and the ability to control and rule our Spirit.

Proverbs 25:28

²⁸ He that hath no rule over his own spirit is like a city that is broken down, and without walls.

Fear torments, stagnates, paralyzes, and stops you from doing anything to help yourself move to the next level and can make you afraid of doing anything about your situation. Fear overpowers you and causes doubts. Fear is also a weapon that is used to trick you. It is used as a weapon to manipulate you and paralyze you, rendering you hopeless and helpless, which handicaps your ability and keeps you in the same mindset and physical state. But the good news is that this is where power, confidence, and trust in GOD are so important. Just ask yourself how badly you want to become stronger, better, and wiser or if you are settling in your ways and satisfied with what you think you are in life. It is extremely critical and important not to stunt your growth; remember God cursed the fig tree because it would not produce.

Matt 21: 18-22

^{18}Early in the morning, as Jesus was on his way back to the city, he was hungry. ^{19}Seeing a fig tree by the road, he went up to it but found nothing on it except leaves. Then he said to it, "May you never bear fruit again!" Immediately the tree withered. ^{20}When the disciples saw this, they were amazed. "How did the fig tree wither so quickly?" they asked. ^{21}Jesus replied, "Truly I tell you, if you have faith and do not doubt, not only can you do what was done to the fig tree, but also you can say to this mountain, 'Go, throw yourself into the sea,' and it will be done. ^{22}If you believe, you will receive whatever you ask for in prayer."

Change, purpose, and evolution are inevitable when it comes to life and who we are as people. I am reminded of the scripture Psalms 28:7, that the Lord is my strength and my shield. Constantly meditating on this scripture has been a great benefit and help pertaining to the reinvention of myself. Speaking this, believing this, and thinking about this have helped solidify my strength. Choosing not to be strong is accepting weakness. It is self-choice because of self-will, and our self-will can get in our way. Some of us are strong-willed and can become very stubborn and set in our own ways. I realized that I had to be relentless when it came to working on myself. Seeing the new you is also important. We have to see ourselves as being successful, operating on another level, and being more than a conqueror. Just ask yourself how you see yourself. What do you see when you look in the mirror? Is it your desire to walk into your new season? Do you believe that it is your time and your turn? Are you excited to see the new you and live the new life that you would want to live? These are literally the types of questions you should be asking yourself, also allowing it to become a mindset of wanting new and seeing yourself do greater things in life. Helping yourself along with helping other people will benefit you along the journey of working out your own. Get the information, learn the knowledge, and use the wisdom when it comes to you and your life. You can live your dream when you write it down and make it plain, believe it, run after it, and make it happen, and you will be able to see the results if you believe it by faith, but you have to put in the work. Facing obstacles and adversaries and fighting your own demons from within tries to stagnate and stop you from this process, but remember you have the power, the insight, the will, and the ability to defeat this and these things to be victorious. Strongholds can be pulled down if you believe, but first, you have to recognize them for what and who they are.

Convince yourself that you are unstoppable and can do all things through Christ that strengthens you; this is the inner strength.

1 John 4:4

Ye are of God, little children, and have overcome them: because greater is he that is in you, than he that is in the world.

Understanding who God is and what He has given you as you abide in Him, and He abides in you is so important for your survival, your purpose, and your life. We are basically predestined to become Better, Stronger, and Wiser. Hopefully, I was able to say something that reached you in a way that will encourage you and assist you in your journey to becoming a better you. May peace, grace, and mercy follow you all the days of your life.

Reuben L. Young Sr.

Reuben L Young Sr. helps individuals discover and live out their purpose. Reuben is a purpose coach, entrepreneur, senior elder, husband, and father. He encourages others to identify their passions, values, and goals.

Reuben has given back to the community by working with at-risk youth and gang intervention in the Los Angeles area through ministry. Reuben also has twenty years of experience working with autistic adults as well as juvenile group homes.

Reuben is the co-CEO and co-founder of Young at Heart Publishing LLC. He puts in a lot of time, work, and effort, also serving as a writing coach with the authors. His goal is to assist and encourage those who aspire to be an author. He helps bring life to the authors' ideas but may need help executing their vision. Reuben is also the owner and founder of True Purpose Coaching Network.

So not only does he help others discover their purpose in writing, but he pushes and encourages others to realize their purpose and potential in so many other areas of their lives.

Reuben is the author of two books:

"The Purpose Formula: Uncover Your Life's Mission and Live with Purpose" and "The Power of Purpose: How Personal Growth Leads to Leadership."

Reuben has served 21 years in ministry as a licensed and ordained pastor and senior elder under the leadership of Chief Apostle Michael L. Rowles at the Wrecking Crew for Christ Holiness Church. There, he has grown and learned how to be a man of standard and integrity.

Contacts Information:

FB-www.facebook.com/Reuben.Young.3154

Website: https://linktr.ee/ReubenLYoung

Email: Truepurposenetwork@gmail.com

Be Authentic

Temika McCann

Let's Break
This Thing Down

LET'S define authenticity: Genuine and real.

What does it mean to be authentic? It means to know yourself.

Take the time to reflect on your morals, values, beliefs, and goals. It is vital that you ask yourself periodically what is essential to you and what you stand for. It is also important that you learn how to accept and embrace your flaws and weaknesses; after all, no one is perfect. Embracing and accepting your imperfections can help you be more authentic, and it will also attract authentic people to you. There was a quote I always live by: "Be You, Be Real, Be Authentic" (Author Unknown). An authentic person will never put on a front to be something they are not. They will be honest in any situation, and they are comfortable with that and never feel the need to explain themselves when they are beginning their true self, which is because they know who they are, period!

Why is it essential to be your authentic self? It makes people feel comfortable around and trust you. Authentic individuals instill a sense of happiness, joy, and peace. When you connect with them, your life will never be the same.

When you are being your authentic self, you have nothing to prove, and actual people truly admire you for that quality. Always remain the same no matter who you are around. When you start switching up when you get around different groups, then people will feel like you are not true to who you are. This quote is something to stand on: "Authenticity is everything, and you don't have to change who you are to fit in."

How to Be Authentic

- Be honest
- Be true to who you are
- Always be genuine
- Be real in any situation
- •Always speak from the heart
- Always be kind
- Always be honest

What does it mean to always be honest? It means they always tell the truth and do right about others. We live in a society where it may seem hard to be yourself, but I found out that it takes a lot of work trying to be someone you are not, so it is best to just be who God created you to be: yourself. The scripture I love to use is Psalm 139:14: "I will praise thee; for I am fearfully and wonderfully made: Marvelous are thy works; And that my soul knoweth right well not try to deceive people or break the law." Never let anyone stop you from being honest because they are dishonest and unwilling to be who they truly are due to being people pleasers. Honesty plays a huge part when interacting with others. If you want to gain their trust, choose honesty over dishonesty, period!

Be Yourself

Life is a journey. As we get older, we start to realize who we are and what we can become. For example, we find out that we have no time to waste, and we must do things that make us happy. When you are authentic, you end up following your heart and not what others want you to do. When you are yourself, you attract and connect with people who not only like to talk with you but love to be around you. Always follow your heart and dreams, and you will never be disappointed. Below are some quotes that can encourage you to be you:

"Knowing yourself is the beginning of all wisdom." –**Aristotle**

"In the end you don't so much find yourself as you find someone who knows who you are." –**Robert Brault**

"Knowing others is intelligence; knowing yourself is true wisdom." –**Lao Tzu**

Support System

Support system and networking are especially important when you are authentic. The reason for this statement is that oftentimes, authentic people are misunderstood and rejected because they dare not level down to fit into any circle or clique; they will always remain solid anytime and anywhere. Building an authentic social support system can hold you accountable. Speak your truth assertively and take daily action towards authenticity on a daily, weekly, and monthly basis, and a support group can help you do that. When you have an authentic support group, you can feel safe, be yourself, and talk about things that bother you without feeling judged. Having a real support group can help you develop better coping strategies when dealing with stressful situations. Always connect with like-minded people, and as you do, your life will never be the same! "Don't let your victories go to your head, or your failures go to your heart."

Living an Authentic Life

When you discover the importance of being your authentic self, you will live a happier life full of possibilities, abundance, and creativity that come to you effortlessly. When you learn to be your true self, you will live a life full of joy, peace, and happiness daily, monthly, and weekly. When you consistently live up to your core values, it leads to self-confidence and true self-worth that will allow you to attract like-minded people who can walk alongside you to help you reach your full potential and create genuine relationships.

Some quotes you can declare over your life on a weekly and daily basis are:

"The purpose of our lives is to be happy." — **Dalai Lama**

"Life is what happens when you're busy making other plans." — **John Lennon**

"Get busy living or get busy dying." — **Stephen King**

Ready To Get Real with Yourself

We live in a world where people say that they are authentic but their actions say something different, and the reason is that they are not keeping it real with who they are. When you get real with yourself, then you can keep it real with others. Being real with yourself and always remembering who you are at your core, the person who dances behind closed doors, is what the world wants. It can take courage to learn how to be real, but when you do, you set yourself free and begin to build a life that brings you joy and meaning. It might not happen overnight, but you can get there.

There are two things we should always be: raw and ready. When you are raw, you are always ready, and when you are ready, you usually realize that you are raw. Waiting for perfection is not an answer. One cannot say, "I will be ready when I am perfect," because then you will never be ready. Rather, one must say,

"I am raw, and I am ready just like this right now, how and who I am." — **C. Joy Bell**

"Opportunity doesn't make appointments; you have to be ready when it arrives." — **Tim Fargo**

"Quit hiding your magic. The world is ready for you."
— **Danielle Doby**

BE YOURSELF

We live in a world where it is a challenge sometimes to be yourself. I have come to the realization that it is a lot harder trying to be someone else. When you are trying to be someone else, you are cheating yourself, and you will not be affected by anyone when trying to be someone that you are not. Life is like a journey; the older we become, the more we must discover who we are and how to set an example and become role models to others in this dark world. Below are quotes I stand on that help me on a daily, weekly, and monthly basis:

"When you are content to be simply yourself and don't compare or compete, everyone will respect you." — **Lao Tzu**

"To shine your brightest light is to be who you truly are." — **Roy T. Bennett**

"Don't compromise yourself - you're all you have." — **John Grisham**

Always Be True

What does it mean to be true? It means that you are your true self. It can mean you do not worry about pleasing other people. You do not care what people think of you, and you have your own ways and standards on how you do things that make you happy. You live a natural life that makes you happy without compromising to fit other people's standards. When you are true to yourself, it allows others to be true to you; it is like a domino effect. When you are true to yourself, you live a life that is fulfilling, filled with joy, and allows you to live an authentic life of purpose. Stay humble at all times. Humility is one of the great examples of an authentic person. So, in other words, it is essential that an authentic person practices being humble. Always be aware of yourself and do not think that you are better than others. Do not overrate your abilities in order to put others down. Humility means that you have discovered yourself and are very content with who you are while working on your shortcomings.

Authentic people show humility in all situations they find themselves in, which is a great attribute to possess. To show that you are authentic, you must show humility to everyone you encounter. This is how we build long-lasting, healthier relationships that will benefit us and others. Below are some quotes that will remind us and encourage you and me to remain humble at all costs:

"A true community is not just about being geographically close to someone or part of the same social web network. It is about feeling connected and responsible for what happens. Humanity is our ultimate community, and everyone plays a crucial role." - **Yehuda Berg**

Staying true to oneself and grounded is more important than money or accomplishments - **Anuel AA**

We must understand that making mistakes is our path to transformation. We are destined to identify them and then move forward to become limitless. Being real is what keeps me humble.

Authentic People Are Doers Rather Than Followers

An authentic person is an individual who does the right things behind closed doors and does not try to follow the trend. Authentic people are concerned with doing the right thing that brings out their true selves by being doers instead of followers. According to the King James Bible,

James 1:22-25

²² "But be doers of the word, and not hearers only, deceiving yourselves. ²³ For if anyone is a hearer of the word and not a doer, he is like a man observing his natural face in a mirror; ²⁴ for he observes himself, goes away, and immediately forgets what kind of man he was. ²⁵ But he who looks into the perfect law of liberty and continues in it and is not a forgetful hearer but a doer of the work, this one will be blessed in what he does."

Authentic people lead by example. They are action-takers, they are genuine at what they do, and they have pure motives while helping others. Being an authentic doer means you do not wait for others to show up. Rather, you create the right positive path for yourself based on your true self. Being a doer means you are always doing the right things that bring about the right results and that create the right impression when interacting with others. A doer can influence others to be doers rather than followers by setting positive examples daily. According to Max Holloway, "I'm not a talker. I'm a doer. "Authentic people are well respected because others can count on them to support them and follow through not with lip service, but through their actions.

Ways To Be Authentic

1. Always be honest
2. Be authentic at all times
3. Always give true advice
4. Share authentic stories that can always uplift others

5. Remain humble
6. Be faithful and kind to others
7. Do not turn on people who help you from a pure place and pure motives
8. Just do you and be you at all costs
9. Lead by example
10. Be honest

Temika McCann

Prophetess Temika McCann gave her life to the Lord at the age of 18, and she did not look back. She birthed the "Passion To Love and Care Ministry Outreach, INC." in 2015, under the mentorship of Dr. W.E. Page at B.T.M.B.C.

Raised in a two-parent Christian home by Judy, between Tommie and Willie McCann, she has six brothers. A devoted wife, mother, servant of the Lord, and Kingdom entrepreneur, she is known as a motivator, encourager, and someone who holds others accountable for their commitments.

Prophetess McCann is actively involved in two outstanding outreach organizations: "Passion To Love and Care Ministry, Inc." and "Touching Lives Outreach," serving communities in Riverside and LA counties. Over the years, she has extended her support to families and children in various countries, including Liberia, Africa,

Pakistan, Kenya, and Nigeria. Her activities range from organizing field trips to Sea World and Disneyland for communities, children, and families to feeding the homeless and assisting those in need, all from a place of pure love.

She embodies the fruit of the Spirit as described in Galatians 5:22-23. She believes in the importance of people becoming their authentic selves to impact the Kingdom of God. She holds an Associate of Arts (AA), Bachelor of Arts (BA), and Master of Science (MS) in Child Development.

Author of six books and a co-author in the #1 bestseller "The Chain Breaking Experience Volume 4," she offers several online courses and holds certifications as a Christian Coach specializing in Mental Health, Health and Wellness, Goal Setting, Accountability, Motivation, Business, and Leadership Coaching.

Prophetess McCann hosts numerous empowerment conferences, revivals, self-growth workshops, and events aimed at helping others reach their full potential. Her passion lies in witnessing women transform into their authentic selves from the inside out rather than the outside in.

She has appeared on several radio stations and TV programs, including G-Map1 Radio Station, Cross TV, the Prophetic Shift Ministry 1460 AM Radio Station, Daughter of the King, Launch the Jesus Initiative, and was chosen among millions of leaders to be part of the National Leadership Conference. Prophetess McCann is authentic, raw, but most importantly, driven by love.

Better Because of It

James Hewitt

Life is about perspective. Your outlook of life will determine your outcome in life. God's intentions were never for life to happen to you but for life to happen through you.

The Bible says in John 10:10: "The thief cometh not but to steal, kill, and destroy; I come that they may have life and that they might have it more abundantly." It is God's desire and plan for man to live a superior quality life in every area. Living life to its fullest overflows with joy, peace, fulfillment, and satisfaction. In the Greek language, the word "life" in this scripture is "Zoe," which means the Godkind of life. Therefore, it is not what happens to you in life (negative circumstances, hurtful situations, hardships, and difficulties) but how you interpret what happens to you in life that will define your destiny.

The Bible says in Job 14:1, "Man that is born of a woman is of a few days and full of trouble." When you understand that trouble will come and go, and bad things will happen, you may not be able to control the circumstances of life. Still, you can control how you view and respond to life circumstances, which will determine the results and outcomes you experience in life.

Motivational speaker and best-selling author Jack Canfield wrote of a formula in his book "The Success Principles." The formula that has helped me get victory and overcome troubling situations and difficult circumstances. Jack Canfield's Formula is E+R = O

E: events

R: Response O: Outcome

This formula means that the events that happen in your life are not as important as how you respond to them. Your response determines the outcome you get, whether it is positive or negative. You can choose to respond in a way that helps you grow and learn from the events or in a way that makes you feel victimized and helpless. One of my mentors, Dr. Manasa Furusa, taught me that I am the only factor I can control in any circumstance. "I'm Better Because of It" is to empower you to take your power back from life. You can let life make you bitter or better.

The choice is yours: "You are the master of your fate, the captain of your soul," as Henry Ford declares. Today, decide, "If it's to be, it's up to me." You have the power to become the change you want to see around you. While you may not have been able to control the hurtful and painful experiences of your past, you can change the trajectory of your future. Your tomorrow does not have to be a repeat of your yesterday because today, you are making up your mind to approach the difficulties and challenges of life with a new perspective.

Empowerment Specialist Dr. Cindy Trimm says, "Life can happen to you, or you can happen to life." No longer will you be a victim of circumstances. Life will no longer happen to you; instead, you will happen to life. I decree that as you read this book, you will experience a paradigm shift, declaring, "I'm Better Because of It." No longer will you look at the devastation, disappointment, and heartache of your life as happening to you, but happening for you. The Bible says in Romans 8:28, "And we know that all things work together for good to them that love God, to them who are the called according to his purpose."

It is amazing to know that God can take the good, the bad, the ugly, and everything in-between to produce something great, masterful, and extraordinary in your life. I am a living example of how you can turn your tragedies into triumphs, scars into stars, pain into purpose, and your mess into a message to bring hope and healing to others.

After being a victim of childhood rape, molestation, physical abuse, living in drug houses, and experiencing rejection by family, leading to placement in the foster care system due to dysfunction, devastation, and disappointment in my life, I attempted suicide three times because I felt like my life had no meaning or sense of purpose. However, when I began to read the Word of God, it changed my thinking. I acquired a new perspective on the negative experiences of my past. No longer do I view what I've been through as working against me; it all was working for me, making me stronger, wiser, and better. Now, I look at every situation in my life as either a blessing or a lesson. I use the circumstances constructively to bring correction, perfection, or direction.

No matter the hardship or difficulty in life, I will always come out of it as a winner, champion, and victorious. Let's consider the biblical story of Joseph. Despite the hardships and heartaches Joseph encountered, from being conspired against, put to death, thrown into a pit, sold into slavery by his brothers, and falsely imprisoned by Potiphar for a lie his wife told, Joseph understood that these events didn't happen to him but for him. They were building, making, and molding him for greatness, preparing him to step into his position of power as second in command next to Pharaoh in the palace (Gen. 50:20): "But as for you, ye thought evil against me; but God meant it unto good, to bring to pass, as it is this day, to save many people alive."

The reason the final outcome of Joseph's tragic and painful story was not one of misery but of great victory is that he learned how to shift his mentality about the misery and dysfunction of his past; he changed his reality. When you change the way you look at a thing, then the thing you are looking at has to change. You can change the trajectory of your future by redefining your past, as I did and Joseph did. We learned that it's not about what you have gone through that defines you but how you look at what you have gone through that makes the difference. Through a transformation of mindset, I learned to turn my tragedies into triumphs and obstacles into opportunities for greatness. I want to share with you how you can do it too.

Step One:

Developing Resilience: Developing resilience involves cultivating the ability to adapt and bounce back from challenges, setbacks, or adversity. It includes building mental and emotional strength to navigate difficult situations and maintain a positive outlook. Resilience also involves learning from experiences, managing stress effectively, and fostering a mindset that promotes growth and well-being.

Steps to Developing Resilience

1. Cultivate a Positive Mindset: Focus on the aspects you can control and maintain an optimistic outlook, even in challenging situations.
2. Build Strong Connections: Develop and nurture supportive relationships with friends, family, or a community. Social support is crucial for resilience.
3. Develop Problem-Solving Skills: Enhance your ability to analyze problems and find effective solutions. Break challenges into smaller, manageable steps.
4. Practice Self-Care: Prioritize your physical and mental well-being through regular exercise, healthy eating, adequate sleep, and relaxation techniques.
5. Learn from Adversity: View challenges as opportunities for growth. Reflect on past experiences, identify lessons learned, and use them to enhance resilience.

6. Set Realistic Goals: Establish achievable objectives and celebrate small victories. This helps build confidence and a sense of accomplishment.
7. Cultivate Adaptability: Embrace change and be open to adjusting your goals and plans. Flexibility is a key component of resilience.
8. Develop Emotional Regulation: Learn to manage and express your emotions in a healthy way. This includes recognizing and accepting feelings without being overwhelmed by them.
9. Maintain a Healthy Lifestyle: Physical health contributes to mental resilience. Exercise, a balanced diet, and adequate sleep positively impact overall well-being. 10. **Seek Professional Support: ** If needed, do not hesitate to consult with mental health professionals for guidance and support in building resilience. Remember, developing resilience is an ongoing process that involves continuous learning and adaptation to life's challenges.

Step Two:

Embracing challenges: "Embracing challenges" means willingly and openly accepting difficulties, obstacles, or hardships in life rather than avoiding or resisting them. It involves adopting a positive and proactive attitude toward challenges, viewing them as opportunities for growth, learning, and personal development. Instead of seeing challenges as setbacks, embracing them implies recognizing the potential for self-improvement and resilience that can result from facing and overcoming obstacles. It is a mindset that encourages individuals to approach challenges with optimism, adaptability, and a willingness to learn from experience.

1. Shift Your Perspective: Reframe challenges as opportunities for growth. See them not as roadblocks but as chances to develop new skills and strengths.

2. Maintain a Positive Mindset: Cultivate a positive attitude even in the face of challenges. Focus on solutions rather than dwelling on problems.

3. Learn from Failures: Embrace the lessons that come with failure. Analyze what went wrong, understand the reasons, and use this knowledge to improve and adapt.

4. Seek Support: Don't hesitate to seek advice or assistance from friends, family, or mentors. Sharing your challenges can provide different perspectives and valuable insights.

5. Stay Flexible: Be open to adjusting your approach. Flexibility is crucial when dealing with challenges, as it allows you to adapt to unexpected circumstances.

6. Develop Resilience: Strengthen your ability to bounce back from setbacks. Resilience is built through facing challenges head-on and learning to navigate through adversity.

7. Celebrate Progress: Acknowledge and celebrate small victories along the way. Recognizing your achievements, no matter how small, reinforces a positive mindset.

8. Continuous Learning: Approach challenges with a mindset of continuous learning. Every experience, whether successful or not, contributes to your personal and professional development.
9. Practice Self-Compassion: Be kind to yourself during challenging times. Understand that everyone faces difficulties, and it is okay not to have all the answers immediately. By incorporating these steps into your approach to challenges, you can develop a more resilient and positive mindset, ultimately contributing to personal growth and success.

Step Three:

Positive Mindset: A positive mindset involves maintaining an optimistic outlook, focusing on solutions rather than problems, and cultivating a hopeful attitude towards challenges and opportunities in life. It is about embracing positivity to enhance resilience and overall well-being.

Steps to Cultivating a Positive Mindset:

1. Practice Gratitude: Regularly acknowledge and appreciate the positive aspects of your life, fostering a sense of thankfulness.
2. Challenge Negative Thoughts: Identify and challenge negative thinking patterns. Replace them with more constructive and optimistic thoughts.

3. Surround Yourself with Positivity: Engage with positive people, environments, and content. Limit exposure to negativity that may affect your mindset.
4. Focus on Solutions: Instead of dwelling on problems, direct your energy towards finding solutions. This proactive approach can shift your mindset.
5. Embrace Change: View change as an opportunity for growth rather than a threat. Adaptability contributes to a positive mindset.
6. Practice Self-Compassion: Treat yourself with kindness and understanding. Accept that everyone makes mistakes and use them as learning opportunities.
7. Positive Affirmations: Use positive statements to reinforce optimistic beliefs about yourself and your abilities.
8. Learn and Grow: See challenges as opportunities to learn and grow. Embrace a mindset of continuous improvement. Consistent effort in these areas can contribute to the development and maintenance of a positive mindset.

Step Four:

Positive self-talk is a practice of using optimistic and affirming language when addressing oneself internally. It involves replacing negative thoughts with constructive and encouraging ones to promote a healthier mindset and boost self-esteem.

The power of positive self-talk is that it is not what people say about you that will make the difference in your life but what you say to yourself about yourself. It was the internal dialog the woman with the issue of blood had with herself that produced her miracle of healing.

Mark 5:25-34 KJV: "And a certain woman, which had an issue of blood twelve years, and had suffered many things of many physicians, and had spent all that she had, and was nothing bettered, but rather grew worse, when she had heard of Jesus, came in the press behind, and touched his garment. For she said, If I may touch but his clothes, I shall be whole. And straightway the fountain of her blood was dried up; and she felt in her body that she was healed of that plague. And Jesus, immediately knowing in himself that virtue had gone out of him, turned him about in the press, and said, Who touched my clothes? And his disciples said unto him, Thou seest the multitude thronging thee, and sayest thou, Who touched me? And he looked round about to see her that had done this thing. But the woman fearing and trembling, knowing what was done to her, came and fell before him, and told him all the truth. And he said unto her, Daughter, thy faith hath made thee whole; go in peace and be whole of thy plague."

Keys for Positive Self-Talk:

1. Avoid Negative Self-Talk Triggers: Identify situations or people that trigger negative thoughts and work on minimizing exposure to them.

2. Replace with Positives: Substitute negative thoughts with positive and affirming statements. Focus on your strengths and accomplishments.
3. Visualization: Picture yourself succeeding in your endeavors. Visualization can enhance confidence and motivation.

Step Five:

Maintain Mental and Emotional Well-being: Maintaining mental and emotional well-being involves actively taking steps to ensure a positive and balanced state of mind. This includes:

1. Self-awareness: Understand your thoughts, feelings, and behaviors to better manage them.
2. Stress management: Develop coping strategies to manage stress and challenges effectively.
3. Healthy relationships: Foster positive connections with others, seeking support and offering support in return.
4. Balanced lifestyle: Prioritize a healthy balance between work, leisure, and self-care activities.
5. Mindfulness: Practice being present in the moment and cultivating a non-judgmental awareness of thoughts and emotions.
6. Physical well-being: Regular exercise, proper nutrition, and adequate sleep contribute to overall mental and emotional health.
7. Positive self-talk: Cultivate a positive internal dialogue to boost self-esteem and resilience.

8. Hobbies and interests: Engage in activities that bring joy and fulfillment, promoting a sense of purpose.//TRUNCATED//
9. Set boundaries: Establish clear boundaries in personal and professional life to avoid burnout and maintain a healthy equilibrium.
10. Seeking help when needed: Reach out to friends, family, or mental health professionals when facing challenges that may impact your well-being.

Step Six:

Developing Coping Skills and Strategies: Coping skills refer to the strategies and techniques individuals use to manage and navigate challenges, stress, or difficult situations effectively. These skills are essential for maintaining emotional well-being and resilience in the face of adversity. Coping skills can be diverse and may include:

1. Being Solution Oriented: Addressing challenges by identifying and implementing solutions.
2. Emotional expression: Articulating and expressing emotions in a healthy and constructive manner.
3. Mindfulness and relaxation techniques: Practices such as meditation, deep breathing, or progressive muscle relaxation to promote calmness.
4. Time management: Organizing and prioritizing tasks to reduce feelings of overwhelm.

5. Humor: Finding humor in situations can provide a different perspective and lighten the mood.
6. Healthy outlets: Engaging in activities like exercise, hobbies, or creative pursuits to channel stress or negative emotions.
7. Cognitive reframing: Changing negative thought patterns into more positive or realistic perspectives.
8. Setting boundaries: Establishing limits to protect personal well-being and manage stressors effectively. Having a range of coping skills allows individuals to adapt to various situations, promoting mental and emotional resilience.

Step Seven:

Cognitive Reframing: Cognitive reframing, also known as cognitive restructuring, is a psychological technique that involves changing the way an individual perceives and interprets a situation, thought, or belief. It aims to shift negative or unhelpful thought patterns into more positive, balanced, or realistic perspectives. The process typically involves:

1. Awareness: Recognizing negative or distorted thoughts.
2. Analysis: Examining the evidence and validity of these thoughts.
3. Challenge: Questioning the accuracy of negative interpretations.

4. Restructuring: Developing alternative, more constructive ways of thinking. For example, if someone perceives a mistake as a complete failure, cognitive reframing will involve helping them see it as a learning opportunity or a stepping stone toward improvement. This technique is often used in cognitive-behavioral therapy (CBT) and can contribute to a more positive and adaptive mindset.

Step Eight:

Healthy Support System: A healthy support system consists of individuals or resources that provide emotional, practical, and sometimes financial assistance in a positive and constructive manner. Elements of a healthy support system include:

1. Emotional Support: People who offer empathy, understanding, and a listening ear during challenging times.
2. Reliability: Individuals you can count on who are consistent and dependable in their support.
3. Positivity: Those who encourage and uplift you, promoting a positive mindset.
4. Respect: Mutual respect and understanding in the relationship, valuing each other's perspectives.
5. Trustworthiness: Being able to trust that your support system has your best interests at heart.

6. Healthy Communication: Open and honest communication that fosters a safe and supportive environment.
7. Diversity: A mix of relationships, including friends, family, and possibly mentors or mental health professionals.
8. Boundaries: Respect for personal boundaries, allowing for a balanced and sustainable support dynamic.
9. Problem-Solving: People who can offer practical advice or help you brainstorm solutions to challenges.
10. Reciprocity: A give-and-take dynamic where support is reciprocated when needed. Having a healthy support system is crucial for mental and emotional well-being, as it provides a network to lean on during both good and challenging times.

Perseverance is not how you start; it's how you finish. The scripture says in Ecclesiastes 9:11-12 KJV, "I returned, and saw under the sun, that the race is not to the swift, nor the battle to the strong, neither yet bread to the wise, nor yet riches to men of understanding, nor yet favor to men of skill; but time and chance happened to them all."

1. Adaptability: Be flexible and willing to adjust your strategies when faced with unexpected challenges
2. Persevere in Patience: Understand that progress takes time, and success often requires ongoing effort. Be patient with the process.

In our journey of becoming Stronger, Better, and Wiser, we must continue to focus, placing our attention and energy on tasks or major goals ahead. And that is to continue to move forward in greatness so that we can walk into the new abundance that God has in store for us.

One of the most important skills you can develop in life is the ability to maintain your focus on your goals and dreams. Many people give up or get distracted by obstacles and challenges, but not you. You know that every setback is an opportunity to learn and grow. You know that every success is a result of your hard work and dedication. You are not a loser or a winner; you are a champion. You are not defeated; you are victorious. You have the power through Christ Jesus to overcome anything with your focused mind and your positive attitude.

JAMES HEWITT

James Hewitt is an Empowerment Specialist, Success Mentor, and Certified Life and Mindset Coach. He is also a prophet, father, and award-winning gospel recording artist. James is the CEO and founder of Mind Your Success Coaching Company, which aims to empower people to achieve their greatness by adopting new mind strategies.

James Hewitt has been preaching the gospel since a young age. He has traveled far and wide to spread the unwavering Word of God, laying his hands on the sick and spreading the message that Jesus is the way, the truth, and the light. James has spent many years under the leadership of Chief Apostle Michael L. Rowles of the Wrecking Crew for Christ Holiness Church.

James Hewitt has been featured on major television networks such as Fox, CBS, and BBC News. He is a singer, songwriter, and Gospel recording artist under the name J. Hewitt. He was previously part of the sensational Gospel R&B music groups

Committed and Anointed 4 Life. James has had the opportunity to share the stage with legendary artists such as Fred Hammon, the DeBarge family, Stevie Wonder, Marvin Sapp, and Tye Tribett. He has made guest appearances on prestigious radio stations such as KJLH (Tammi Mac Show), Kevin Nash Praise Radio, NTYM Radio, and Real Urban Radio Network. James has also made many guest appearances on television networks such as The Cross TV Network, Prayer Saved My Life, Jesus is Our Jubilee, and OCN television network.

James is a multi-nominated award-winning artist and a 2021 finalist of the Gospel Choice Music Awards show and the Praise Factor Season 14 Awards. His mission through his music is to inspire hope, healing, and positive change through Jesus Christ.

Contact Information:

FB: James Hewitt, J.Hewitt

Email: mindyoursuccess86gmail.com

Notes

Scriptures were used from Biblegateway.com; All versions

Made in the USA
Middletown, DE
17 March 2024